HAWAII

A Turner Educational Services, Inc. book. Based on the Portrait of America television series created by R.E. (Ted) Turner.

Library of Congress Number: 86-17812

Library of Congress Cataloging in Publication Data

Thompson, Kathleen.
 Hawaii.

 (Portrait of America)
 "A Turner book."
 Summary: Discusses the history, economy, culture, and future of Hawaii. Also includes a state chronology, pertinent statistics, and maps.
 1. Hawaii—Juvenile literature. [1. Hawaii]
I. Title. II. Series: Thompson, Kathleen.
Portrait of America.
DU623.25.T57   1986   996.9   86-17812

ISBN 0-8174-451-6   hardcover library binding

ISBN 0-8114-6777-5   softcover binding

Cover Photo: Hawaii Visitors Bureau

 2 3 4 5 6 7 8 9 0   96 95 94 93 92

★ ★ ★ ★ ★

Portrait of AMERICA

HAWAII

Kathleen Thompson

RSVP
RAINTREE
Steck-Vaughn
P U B L I S H E R S
The Steck-Vaughn Company

Austin, Texas

CONTENTS

Introduction

Hawaii, the Aloha State.

"You just have to see it to believe it. I think this is probably a little bit of what heaven's going to be like."

Hawaii: sugar, pineapple, orchids, Pearl Harbor.

"We want to preserve the past, use what we have learned, use those pieces of the past for the future. And I think we can."

Hawaii, the only state that is not on the United States mainland, is also the only state that was once a kingdom. It is full of history, just as it is full of beauty and sunshine.

Hawaii is 132 islands and dozens of cultures. It is a place where the rest of this country goes to play. And it is also a people who are determined not to take the mistakes of its past into its bright, sunny future.

Islands Out of the Sea

For millions of years, lava has poured up out of underwater volcanoes, building and shaping islands in the middle of the Pacific Ocean. One hundred and thirty-two of them form the chain of islands we call Hawaii.

Until about twelve hundred years ago, no one lived on the islands. Then, in about A.D. 750, they were settled by a group of people called Polynesians. (Some say that the Polynesians came even earlier, about two thousand years ago.) For the next thousand years, a strong family-based culture grew up in Hawaii. But the islands were not united. There were smaller units of government, sometimes covering a single island, sometimes including several islands.

It was a man named Kamehameha who brought the islands

Kilauea volcano, on the island of Hawaii, is shown
during one of its many eruptions.

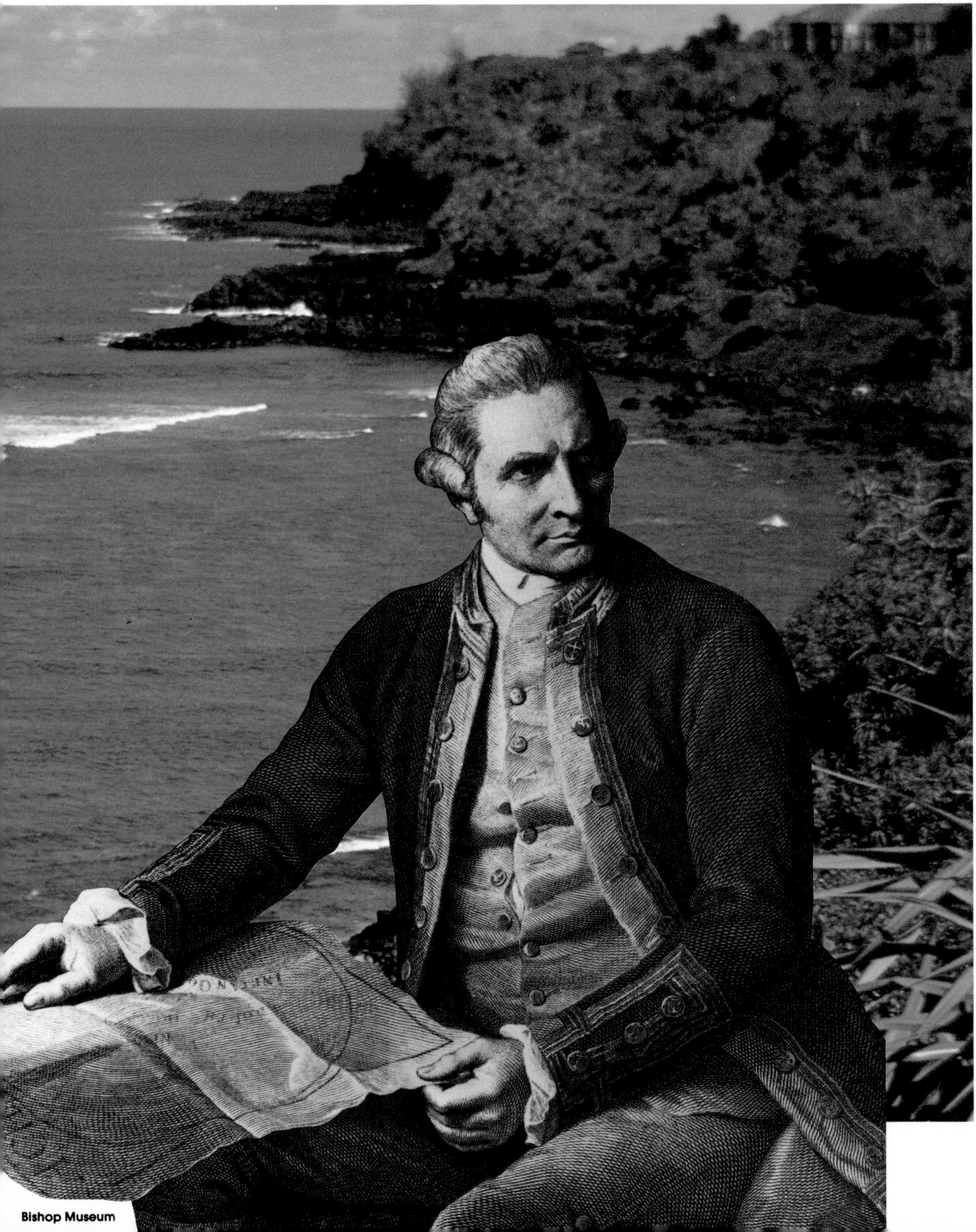

Hawaii Visitor's Bureau

Bishop Museum

together. He was chief of a group of people on the western coast of the largest island, Hawaii. Kamehameha was a strong leader and a remarkable man. But he probably would not have been able to unite the islands if it hadn't been for another man, Captain James Cook.

Captain Cook was an English explorer. In January of 1778, he "discovered" the Hawaiian Islands. When he and his men first arrived, they were treated with great respect. They enjoyed the hospitality of the islands for several days and then went on to America. On their way back to the South Pacific, they stopped again.

Again, Cook and his men were treated well. But they seemed to have overstayed their welcome. After about two weeks, one of their small boats was stolen. Cook overreacted. He took a dozen armed men ashore to kidnap a chief and hold him hostage until the boat was returned. The islanders, understandably, resisted. Cook and several of his men were killed.

For some time after that, Europeans left the Hawaiian Islands alone. But Hawaii's position as a way station between Asia and America was too attractive. Eventually, trading ships began stopping regularly.

To the Europeans, Hawaii offered a place to renew supplies on their long journeys. It also offered sandalwood, which was in great demand at the time. To Hawaii, the Europeans offered a variety of diseases that the islanders could not fight and guns.

It was the guns that made all the difference to Kamehameha. He and his people traded for them and then used them to conquer the other islands.

Kamehameha set up his own governors to rule the individual islands. He took control of all trade. He hired Europeans to work for him as advisers.

Kamehameha's power was pretty much unchallenged from 1795 until he died in 1819. Then, two of his wives made important changes in Kamehameha's system of government. Many of the old rituals were discarded. But his dynasty continued. His son, Liholiho, became king—Kamehameha II.

On the left-hand page is a nineteenth-century engraving of Captain James Cook against the background of the coastline of the island of Kauai.

The picture above depicts an early nineteenth-century missionary preaching to the islanders.

About this time, American missionaries began to come to Hawaii to convert the islanders to Christianity. They became an important influence on the culture of the people. The mission leaders became advisers to the government. These missionaries were Protestants. An early attempt by Roman Catholic missionaries to bring their creed into the islands was unsuccessful and, in 1831, the government forced the priests to leave.

Another important influence was outside industry. In 1835, the first permanent sugar plantation went into operation. It was owned, not by the Hawaiians, but by an American group, Ladd & Company.

In 1840, Hawaii adopted its first constitution. In 1842, the United States recognized the Kingdom of Hawaii as an independent government. At this time, all the land in Hawaii was owned by the king. He allowed

A sugar plantation on the island of Oahu.

others to use and live on the land, and he collected rents.

Then, in 1848, the land was divided up among King Kamehameha III and the major chiefs. They returned most of it to the government, and it was sold to or claimed by Hawaiian citizens. That was the beginning of private property in Hawaii.

When Captain Cook first came to Hawaii, there were 300,000 people living on the islands. But the European diseases had, by about 1850, reduced the number to fewer than 75,000. As the sugar plantations grew, the owners began to bring in workers from other countries.

The first to come were the Chinese. By the mid-1860s, there were more Chinese males in the islands than white males. The Japanese began to come over in 1868. By 1887, they were coming in large numbers. Later, the plantations brought in Filipinos, Koreans, Portuguese, and Puerto Ricans.

As the sugar plantations became more and more powerful, there was conflict with the government. The plantations were owned by non-Hawaiians. The owners' interest in the island was in making money. The use of the land for growing sugar had pretty thoroughly destroyed the small farm economy of the Hawaiians.

It was the same kind of situation that brought so much poverty and cultural destruction in Puerto Rico, in the American South, and in many places around the world.

Camera Hawaii, Inc.

13

In 1887, a group of the leading taxpayers in Hawaii led a revolution against King Kalakaua. They forced him to accept a new constitution. Under the new constitution the king had little or no power. The power was now in the hands of the property owners, most of whom were white. Two-thirds of the native population were denied the right to vote.

The Reform Party, besides forcing the new constitution, began to work with the United States for closer ties. They gave the United States exclusive rights to the use of Pearl Harbor as a naval station. They started talking about Hawaii becoming part of the United States.

In 1891, Kalakaua died. His sister, Liliuokalani became queen. She was determined to regain power for the monarchy and for the Hawaiian people. She tried to get rid of the Reform Constitution and create a new one.

She was stopped. Nine Americans, two Britons, and two Germans led a revolution against her. They were backed up by the United States minister to Hawaii, John L. Stevens, and by the commander of a U.S. warship stationed at Honolulu. American troops came ashore from the warship and Queen Liliuokalani surrendered. She expressed the hope that the U.S. Congress would not approve of the support Minister Stevens had given the revolutionaries.

The revolutionaries immediately tried to get the United States to take over Hawaii. But President Grover Cleveland ordered an investigation. He decided that the revolutionaries would not have succeeded without Stevens' help. He ordered that the monarchy be restored.

However, the revolutionaries refused. They set up their own government and appointed Sanford B. Dole as president.

Queen Liliuokalani and her followers tried a counterrevolution in January of 1895. But they did not have the force necessary. They failed, and the queen was arrested for treason. She was sentenced to five years hard labor and a fine of $5,000. Later her sentence was reduced, and she was restored to citizenship in November 1896.

In 1898, the United States

Queen Liliuokalani.

annexed Hawaii. It was now no longer an independent country, but a territory of the United States. Sanford B. Dole was appointed governor.

The sugar growers were happy because, as part of the United States, there would be no tariff on the sale of their sugar in the United States.

By this time, the original Hawaiians were becoming a smaller and smaller part of the population. And political and economic power, as Hawaii entered the twentieth century, would remain in the hands of the men who had led the rebellion against Queen Liliuokalani. By 1910, a group of five companies produced and marketed 75 percent of the sugar in Hawaii. By 1933, they controlled 96 percent. They also controlled most of the territory's banking, insurance, utilities, transportation, and wholesale and retail business. As a result, they also controlled politics.

And they were white.

But increasingly, another group was making itself felt. The children of the Japanese brought over to work on the plantations were American citizens. They expected, and were guaranteed by the American Constitution, full rights. By 1936, one out of every four voters in Hawaii was Japanese-American.

And on December 7, 1941, the Japanese attacked Pearl Harbor. The United States was at war with Japan.

Hawaii was placed under martial law. A curfew was enforced. The military took over the courts and law enforcement. These harsh measures were taken because the United States government doubted the loyalty of Japanese-Americans both in Hawaii and on the mainland. In California, Americans of Japanese descent were put in concentration camps. In Hawaii, there were too many Japanese to do that.

On the right-hand page is a photograph of Pearl Harbor on December 7, 1941. The soldiers below are shown in a welcoming home ceremony after the war.

STATEHOOD.

House Sends
Bill to Ike

These doubts about loyalty were completely wrong. One proof of this was the 100th Battalion, a volunteer group of Japanese-American soldiers who fought in Europe and became the most highly decorated unit in the United States Armed Forces.

Many of the members of the 100th Battalion came back to form the center of a group that challenged white political power in the islands after the war. By 1954, one out of every two members of the territorial legislature was an American of Japanese ancestry. In 1959, Hawaii became a state.

After statehood, Hawaii changed tremendously. Sugar and pineapple growing, though still important, no longer dominated the economy. Tourism began to bring about four million people a year to the islands.

The island paradise of the Polynesians had gone through many difficult changes. Now it was taking its place in the modern world as a state, as an ethnic melting pot, as an increasingly varied economy . . . and as an island paradise.

On the left-hand page, against a background of Hanauma Bay, is a girl holding a newspaper that announces Hawaii's statehood. At the left is a photograph of members of the 100th Battalion, the first all-nisei combat unit in World War II.

Palace of Earth

"I'm a modern Hawaiian, and I have ancestors from many parts of the world. So I am half Hawaiian. If you're born even a little Hawaiian, you're Hawaiian at heart."

Professor Rubellite Kawena Johnson's Hawaii is a mixture of old and new, a combination of what was here before the coming of human beings and what has been brought here by a dozen different strains of the human race.

To Ruby Johnson, the old has a special meaning, especially in a eucalyptus grove on Oahu. There, a heap of rocks brings back to her the rituals and customs of her ancestors.

"We often think that kings, today, are born in palaces. And I think of this as an ancient palace for the kings to be born. . . . Earth Mother is a goddess, the sky above is Sky Father, so this is our house. . . ."

This feeling of closeness to the earth is a part of all the old Hawaiian customs. When the Christian missionaries came, the old customs were seen as primitive. Eventually, the old religion was outlawed. Today, Hawaiians like Ruby Johnson try to rediscover the past and to find what was lost.

"The rocks, the earth, the soil, the air, the water, those are all the things that compose the human being. We are born from these basic elements, so we have nothing to fear."

In Hawaii, as in most places, there is much to be grateful for in the new and much to be learned from the old.

On the right-hand page is a photograph of Professor Rubellite Kawena Johnson. The photo below shows a woman teaching her granddaughter the art of weaving.

Hawaii Visitor's Bureau

Robert Elfstrom

21

Sugar, Pineapples, and Beauty

When you think of Hawaii, you probably think of beautiful islands where tourists wear necklaces of orchids, swim on sandy beaches, and eat exotic foods. If so, you're right.

Tourism is Hawaii's leading industry. About four million people a year come to enjoy the beauty of the islands. They bring about $3 billion a year into the economy.

This presents Hawaii with an interesting problem. It is the natural beauty of the state that brings in the people. And the more people come, the more difficult it is to preserve that beauty. But so far, Hawaii seems to be doing a pretty good job of it.

In all, Hawaii has 132 islands. On Oahu, visitors can enjoy the big-city atmosphere of Honolulu, the high-rise hotels,

Kaanapali Beach, on the island of Maui.

clubs, and restaurants of Waikiki Beach. On Maui, there is a quieter, less developed feeling. Most of the smaller islands are determined to keep their natural beauty and traditional culture alive.

The second largest element in the Hawaiian economy is the U.S. military. The Pacific Fleet is responsible for defending U.S. interests in an area that covers about 50 percent of the earth's surface. Its presence in Hawaii is a big one.

There are about fifty military installations in Hawaii. Pearl Harbor shipyard is the largest single industrial employer in the state.

After tourism and the military in the Hawaiian economy, comes sugar. Sugar is the major agricultural product. And food processing, primarily sugar process-

The warships below were photographed during allied forces' exercises in the mid-1980s. Below, left, are members of the Marine Guard Detachment at Pearl Harbor.

U.S. Navy

ing, is the major manufacturing activity.

The influence of sugar and pineapple is far reaching. About 50 percent of the people working on the island of Kauai, for example, are connected with the sugar industry. The island of Lanai is owned by Castle and Cooke, the parent company of Dole Pineapple.

All forms of manufacturing account for almost two-thirds of the value of goods produced in Hawaii every year. Food processing accounts for almost one-half of that. Most of that processing is sugar and pineapple.

Agriculture accounts for about one-third of the value of goods produced in the state. Most of the agricultural activity is, again, sugar and pineapple raising. It's done on large plantations. There are very few small farms in Hawaii.

Pineapples (below) take approximately eighteen to twenty-two months to ripen.

U.S. Navy

Dole Company

There are also large cattle ranches. The cattle are not raised for export, however. The beef is sold to restaurants and markets in the state.

Another important area of agricultural activity is flower growing. And there are smaller crops such as coffee, macadamia nuts, and fruits.

For a long time, the economy of Hawaii was much too dependent on the sugar and pineapple plantations. Tourism and military spending broke that hold. But now, there are those who are concerned that the state's economy is becoming too tied to tourism.

And it's hard to turn your back on a goose that's laying golden eggs by the dozen.

The photograph at the bottom shows Waikiki Beach, one of Hawaii's best-known tourist attractions. Before pineapples are ready for canning, they are washed in pure water. Flower growing (right-hand page) represents a major portion of Hawaii's agriculture.

Dole Company

Hawaii Visitor's Bureau

Cruisin'

"You ready to go downhill?"

With those words, Bob Kiger starts off one of the simplest, smoothest, and most delightful tourist attractions in Hawaii. For two and a half hours, he and his group will cruise on their bicycles from the top of a volcanic mountain down to the sea —downhill all the way.

"All my life I worked so hard selling things, and here's something I don't have to sell. People just want it. They want as much of it as they can get. They want to go downhill."

These two photographs show Bob Kiger and his dog Maui.

Photos courtesy Bob Kiger

28

Somehow, it seems like a very Hawaiian thing to do. Or at any rate, it's the sort of thing for which people go to Hawaii. To relax. To take it easy. Downhill all the way.

"The first time I rode a bike was nothing like this. This is a cruise. I mean, lookit, effortless. What could be more visual than cruising through this eucalyptus forest right here? Smelling it. Smell it! Just fantastic. Like cruising through a tube of mentholatum."

Before Bob Kiger came to Hawaii, he was a video producer in Los Angeles. He left that city when they started taking out the orange groves and putting in the pavement. And now he provides his own special Hawaiian experience to other people who come here from the hurry and bustle and tension of the cities.

"I think life is a downhill cruise and all we're really doing is trying to learn to deal with it. And what we teach people to do here is to give up their fears and go with it. Perfect. And a lot of people never forget it."

On the left-hand page, Bob Kiger and a group of cyclists are shown at Paia, the base of the downhill cruise. The photograph below shows a group ready to start down the mountain. Below, left, is a photo of the group cruising down Haleakala Highway. The group will travel thirty-eight miles in about three hours.

The Old Plantation

"We've been here for one hundred years, and we have ties to the past. We are still a family company, and our reasons for development may not be only the dollar. We want to be sure that we do something that's in keeping with what we have here in Wimeia, the character of the town."

Sugar is still important in Hawaii, but it is not nearly as important as it once was. Many of the old plantations have been closed. The landowners have left, returning to the mainland. But Mike Faye is one who chose to stay.

Mike can't make a living growing sugar on the plantation his grandfather owned. But he's decided to use it in a different way. He's going to give tourists the opportunity to live for a while on an old plantation.

"We have what's left of a sugar plantation. We've got the camp, we've got the old mill building, we've got the shops. We've got the churches on our property. We've got the manager's house. For us to tear all that down and start from scratch will make us look like any other place. We think we can create something that nobody else has."

So the carpenters have come in and repaired sagging porches. The plasterers have gone to work on the walls. The plumbers have put in modern kitchens and bathrooms. It won't be quite the way it was when the workers lived here. If it were, the tourists wouldn't come. But something will be saved of the past.

The house below is kept as it was many years ago to give tourists an idea of what living on an old sugar plantation was like. On the right-hand page is Mike Faye against the background of one of the remodeled cottages where tourists can stay on the plantation.

"The feeling one gets going through a camp is special. When I go through there, being raised around the camp, I get that same feeling. Well, the camp is alive. . . . It's a feeling of community. When people leave here we want them to leave with a good feeling and a feeling that they have experienced a way of life that is not there anymore."

The Colors of Hawaii

It's not a tapestry. The colors are too bright for that. It's not any kind of weaving. The colors are splashed on, not intricately woven through. And for all its history, it has a new feeling to it. Hawaii is a garden, a painting, an aloha shirt.

In most places on earth, human life goes back far beyond history. We can only guess at its hidden origins. But Hawaii is different. Hawaii is a group of volcanic islands in the middle of the Pacific Ocean. The land itself is new. And the first people who ever lived on it came here late in the history of humanity.

To the lush green and bright flowers of the islands, the Polynesians brought their own color. And each group that came after them—Japanese, Chinese, Portuguese, Filipino,

The flowers at the edge of this lily pond are Traveler's palms.

Korean, European, American—added another shade. There has been some blending. One culture has mingled a little on the edges with each other culture. But each color has also kept its brilliance, its own special quality.

Take music. Music and dancing have always been a part of Hawaii. The graceful hula was a way the original Hawaiians prayed, spoke to their gods. But the ukulele, that very Hawaiian instrument, was created from a small guitar brought to the Islands by the Portuguese. And the favorite song of Hawaii—"Aloha Oe," written by Queen Liliuokalani—has a beautiful, haunting melody, but one that owes more to Tin Pan Alley than to the traditional music of Hawaii.

The muumuu—a loose, brightly colored dress worn all over the islands—was introduced by the American missionaries. And even the most traditional of European clothing takes on a special quality in Hawaii.

In everything from food to religion to language, there is this feeling of a bright, colorful mixture. It is as though the culture of Hawaii were trying to match the birds and flowers, the sparkling sand of the beaches, and the deep blue of the ocean.

The woman in the photograph below is making leis, the traditional flower necklace of Hawaii. On the right-hand page, hula dancers are performing native dances for tourists.

37

Aina

"Because I'm part Japanese and Chinese and doing this taro trip, which is sort of Hawaiian. . . . I just think of myself as a local boy who's working for a living down here."

In most places, a local boy working for a living probably wouldn't be planting taro plants under the surface of the water next to a waterfall while a friend played a flute for good luck. But, of course, Hawaii isn't most places.

"When I'm in the patch, it's so beautiful. And you look in the back, there's a nice waterfall. On the two sides are the mountains. And the ocean's in the front with a cool breeze. So you feel like you have no worries and just concentrate on working."

It sounds like a wonderful way to make a living, and it is. It's also a sign of the way many people in Hawaii work with the land and not against it. There may be more efficient ways to plant taro, but Eric Zane has found in the traditional rituals of planting a way to share in the beauty as well as the productivity of the land.

"You have to respect the land. Respect is automatic once you just love the land, the 'Aina,' they called it."

At the right is Eric Zane against the background of a taro patch in Waipio Valley.

In another part of Hawaii, Kepa Maly, a park ranger, explains one of the reasons that Hawaiians have a special relationship to the land.

"We usually think of earth as being eons old. You know, it's long before and long after us in most cases. But anyone could come to Hawaii and step on earth that's younger than they are."

The earth is young here because it is constantly being created by underwater volcanic activity. Many scientists believe that another island is right now being formed in Hawaii and that someday there will be 133 Hawaiian Islands.

"Many people haven't really thought of the earth as being fragile, but I think Hawaii is a showcase in fragility."

That is Hawaii. It's beautiful. It's delicate. It needs and deserves to be taken care of.

Shown against the background of Hawaii Volcanoes National Park is ranger Kepa Maly.

Robert Elfstrom

Into the Future

Once Hawaii was a country of people who fished and grew only what they needed to live on. It was a simple, peaceful way of life. Then came the plantations. Hawaiians worked on other people's land growing other people's crops. Most of the money that was made left the islands. Sugar and, later, pineapple were the only economy.

Gradually, military spending and tourism began to change all that. Today, tourism holds first place in the economy of Hawaii. And that is the problem of Hawaii's future.

To begin with, there are few high-paying jobs in the tourist industry. Most of the people employed in this area are clerks, waiters, entertainers—service people. The wages offered by high tech industries and management corporations

The shoreline at Waikiki Beach.

are just not available in Hawaii.

And then, many Hawaiians feel that using their most treasured rituals and customs to entertain the tourists is not good for the culture or for the people.

Finally, the natural beauty that draws tourists is in danger. Every high-rise hotel that is built to house tourists takes a little bit away from what the people of the island treasure—and the tourists come to see. Hawaii is full of endangered species. And the freshwater supply is very fragile.

But Hawaii is approaching the problems of the future with ingenuity and confidence. Although the tourist industry will probably always be important to Hawaii's economy, the state is making attempts to develop other sources of income and employment. One example is the growth of *aquaculture.* Aquaculture is the commercial raising of plants and animals that live in water. These water farmers grow, among other things, fish, oysters, and shrimp.

There is more light industry now than at any time in the past. And Hawaii is trying to develop its own energy sources. There are many experiments with solar energy, wind power, and gasohol.

But just as important as these attempts to vary the economy are the moves to preserve the Hawaiian culture. Hawaiians have retained their pride in their traditions. And that is good, not only for the people, but also for the islands because those traditions include a deep respect for the land.

It seems that the best hope for Hawaii's future is for this state to become more and more what it is—Hawaii.

Important Historical Events in Hawaii

750 About this time, Polynesians come from other Pacific islands and settle Hawaii.

1778 Captain James Cook visits Hawaii on his way from the South Pacific to the northwest coast of America.

1795 King Kamehameha I brings all the islands except Kauai and Niihau together under his rule.

1810 Kauai and Niihau become part of Kamehameha's kingdom.

1819 Kamehameha I dies. Two of his wives make changes in the ritual basis of the monarchy. Kamehameha II takes power.

1820 Protestant missionaries come to the island to convert the Hawaiians to Christianity.

1835 The first permanent sugar plantation is built by Ladd & Company.

1840 Hawaii adopts its first constitution.

1852 Chinese workers begin to arrive to work on the sugar plantations.

1868 Japanese workers begin to come to Hawaii to work on the plantations.

1887 The major landowners and taxpayers, mostly white, force King Kalakaua to approve a new constitution, which denies voting rights to most of native population. The new party gives the United States rights to use Pearl Harbor as a naval station.

1891 Queen Liliuokalani comes to power and begins to fight the control of the white minority.

1893 A rebellion of white leaders backed by the U.S. Minister and a U.S. warship overthrows Queen Liliuokalani.

1894 After President Cleveland refuses to annex Hawaii, the leaders of the rebellion declare Hawaii a republic.

1898 Hawaii becomes a U.S. possession.

1900 The Territory of Hawaii is established.

1910 A group of five large companies controls 75 percent of Hawaii's sugar crop.

1927 The first airplane flight is made from the mainland to Hawaii.

1933 The five large companies control 96 percent of the sugar crop and most of the banking, insurance, utilities, and transportation in Hawaii.

1941 The Japanese attack Pearl Harbor.

1950 The legislature of the Territory of Hawaii approves a constitution which will go into effect at statehood.

1959 Hawaii becomes a state.

1960s The tourist industry begins to boom.

1975 A massive tidal wave and two earth quakes hit Hawaii causing enormous damage.

Hawaii Almanac

Nickname. The Aloha State.

Capital. Honolulu.

State Bird. Hawaiian Goose.

State Flower. Hibiscus.

State Tree. Candlenut.

State Motto. *Ua mau ke ea o ka aina i ka pono* (The life of the land is perpetuated in righteousness.)

State Song. Hawaii Ponoi.

State Abbreviations. Ha. (traditional); HI (postal).

Statehood. August 21, 1959, the 50th state.

Government. Congress: U.S. senators, 2; U.S. representatives, 2. **State Legislature:** senators, 25; representatives, 51. **Counties:** 4.

Area. 6,450 sq. mi. (16,705 sq. km.), 47th in size among the states.

Elevation. Highest: Mauna Kea, 13,796 ft. (4,205 m). **Lowest:** sea level.

Population. 1980 Census: 964,691 (25% increase over 1970), 39th in size among the states. **Density:** 150 persons per sq. mi. (58 persons per sq. km.). **Distribution:** 87% urban, 13% rural. **1970 Census:** 769, 913.

Economy. Agriculture: sugar cane, pineapples, coffee, macadamia nuts, fruits, melons, vegetables, nuts. **Fishing Industry:** tuna. **Manufacturing:** sugar, sugar products, food products, clothing, printed materials, furniture, wood products. **Mining:** stone.

Places to Visit

Aloha Tower in Honolulu.

Barking Sounds on Kauai.

Kaimu Black Sand Beach on Hawaii.

Kapiolani Park, near Honolulu.

Kealakekua Bay on Hawaii.

Nuuanu Pali on Oahu.

Pearl Harbor on Oahu.

Polynesian Culture Center on Oahu.

Sea Life Park on Oahu.

Waimea Canyon on Kauai.

Annual Events

Hula Bowl football game in Honolulu (January).

Hawaiian Open International Golf Tournament on Oahu (January and February).

Island Cruise and Merrie Monarch Festival in Hilo (April).

Lei Day, statewide (May).

50th State Fair on Oahu (June-July).

Hula Festival in Honolulu (August).

Aloha Festival on Hawaii, Kauai, Maui, Moloki, and Oahu (September-October).

International Surfing Championships at Makaha Beach, Oahu (December).

Hawaii Counties

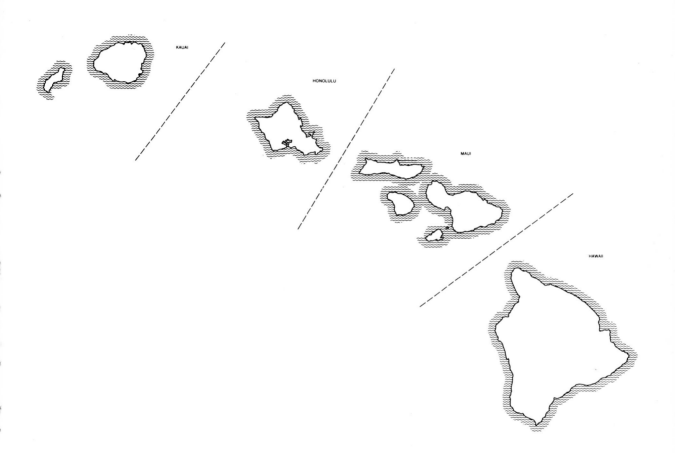

KAUAI

HONOLULU

MAUI

HAWAII

INDEX